Gordon Hoyles

as read at Richard's events
The Red Lion, Manningtree

To Lesley

Wishing

[signature]   26. 08. 2021

INTRODUCTION

They may be enjoyed but sometimes little poems spoken come with the shock and surprise of a good sneeze, or like shooting stars, glow powerfully but fleeting.

I just thought you may like to consider some of them again if they lingered on a page. So, we published.

We thank Richard for creating an opportunity to perform and share a platform every second Tuesday of the month at The Red Lion, Manningtree. Long may it continue.

Strangely the old ones taught the young ones with insistence difficulty test and punishment and as strangely the young ones accepted the wisdom as without noticing they became the old ones and on the plateau they couldn't find what the training had been for so strangely they taught the young ones with insistence difficulty test and punishment and as strangely the young ones accepted the wisdom as without noticing they became the old ones and on the plateau they couldn't find what the training had been for so strangely they taught the young ones with insistence difficulty test and punishment and as strangely the young ones accepted the wisdom as without noticing they became the old ones and on the plateau they couldn't find what the training had been for so strangely they taught the young ones with insistence difficulty test and punishment and as strangely the young ones accepted the wisdom as without noticing they became the old ones and on the plateau they couldn't find what the training had been for so strangely they taught the young ones with insistence difficulty test and punishment and as strangely the young ones accepted the wisdom as without noticing they became the old ones and on the plateau they couldn't find what the training had been for so strangely the old ones taught the young ones with insistence difficulty test and punishment and as strangely the young ones accepted the wisdom as without noticing they became the old ones and on the plateau they couldn't find what the training had been

9th May 2017

STENA BRITANNICA

Suddenly she's throbbing
as the 46,000-horsepower vibrator
dildos into action.

It's steady as she goes
until the shaking frenzied climax
of coming in the port.

UP THE GARDEN PATH

Tall and elegant with arms raised gently waving
bouquets. Skin so tight, full and smooth; not a
wrinkle, nor a pimple. Just clean-limbed
perfection calmly and quietly standing naked
before me.

The graceful eucalyptus
A beautiful Eve in Beth Chatto's garden.

13th June 2017

HAIKU 1

Awaited promise.

The uneaten ice cream melts.

Journey never made.

– – – – – – – – – – – – – –

HAIKU 2   version 2

Wishing's the first thing.

Rubbing the lamp brings genie.

Ask the dreamcatcher.

LOVE STORY

We talked and talked of this and thats
of parrots pigs and pussycats
and doing joined- up writing.
I said how nice was her new hat
and everything was going fine.

We made a plan for meeting hence
when we would have vagina time
and peace bestowed by fearless trust
and all forgiving understanding
that so enhances mundane lust
and doing joined-up writing.

Yes everything was going fine
and then the romance ended
well it had to 'cos she ate all my favourite
biscuits.

There was an old spider called Bruce
Who, spotting a fly buzzing loose,
Said, "you're looking much thinner
So, please come to dinner
And I'll let you swing on my noose".

11th July 2017

I had to catch up with my grandaughter's reading.

THE FAMOUS FIVE ABRIDGED

One day when Aunt Fanny was out Julian finally got the proof that George was a girl when he came upon Timothy licking her all over.

"I like Dick a lot," George said, "but I love Tim, love Tim so much I couldn't be without him for a minute."

Little Anne turned bright red with all the excitement of such a thrilling, top secret adventure, and was bursting to tell what she knew.

George said, "You'll get a good kicking if you do."

GENERAL ELECTION 2017

Surprise surprise
The nobodies' shouted "game on".
And the everybodies cheered and danced.

It was a strange game, a bit like quiddich,
goings on in all dimensions and all directions,
on the bus, texting, cyber, you name it
every which way foul blows were delivered.

At the final whistle the nobodies scored 318
whilst the everybodies scored 262.

The captain of the everybodies declared "We won."
"We won" he shouted," it's a rout."
"It's obvious who won" he said through his beautiful smile.
"It's pointless, the captain of the nobodies must go.
Get out of my way, I have a clear mandate."
and at the same time demanded another game rematch.
And the everybodies cheered and danced and went hysterical
when smiling, he chanted," the nobodies' can't be allowed to carry
on".

The nobodies bemused, wondered why he hadn't been sectioned.

The media jabbering their rabble babble rabble babble rabble
babble spread the virus.

Perhaps it's fake news and they've all been interfered with by the
Russians.?

And bike-shedding.

8th August 2017

LISTENING TO THE GROWN-UPS

And me and little Blossom playing at house overheard the grown-ups talking.

"The oyster failed to lure the seed," said one

"Might as well stitch it up" said ranting agony aunty all sourness. "And just suck the lollipops."

"Be quiet you two."

Then they said, "they say they may bring back the horse and farmyard smells and knee-deep in poo to grow the roses."

"Be quiet you two" they shouted.

"And we all have to take some HS2 or nobody will be able to go" they said

"Be quiet you two"

And we're all going all battery and no nuclear.

Be quiet you two.

So me and little Blossom hearing some bongoes feeding drifted away and tried to find some 'lectric.

JOURNEYING

The brain's understanding is performing all alive to eternity.

phssssss
What shall we do   ?
Where will we go?
What is it for?
Is there some more?
Want something new.
What a ta do.
Where'll we go?
Where'll we go?
Ma longa me
whirl we go
whirl we go.
Ma longa me
off on a spree
often a spree
esprit
esprit.
Crossing of points
let in it, let in it
letting it go,
letting it go,
ma longga me
ma longga me
to got to go soon
got to be done
got to be done
waddling womb
to me to you to me to you
can it be true
somehow it grew
what shall we do
whirl we go
over to you
what a ta do
crossing of points
en nem men knee
en nem men knee
when'll we see
en nem en nem en nem en nem
en em ma nem
en em ma nem ma knee
to do
what a ta do
go somewhere new

ma longa me
ma longga me
what is it for
implore explore
what's it for?
we're all we know
we roll we know
we roll we know
where roll we go
what a ta do
snuggling up
snug gul lin nup
over to you
hen'll we be
then'll we see
when'll
then'll
what'll
whirl we
whirl we be
what a ta do
what is it for
is there some more

phisssssssss

10

12th September 2017

HEARING DIFFICULTIES   *Performance Piece*

Watching   waiting
Not so much chasing
as the beautiful butterfly
flicks from head to head
sucking at the stems
till the pollen is shed.

The butterfly watcher
(the voyeur of the piece)
nervous, too tense to move,
afraid to breathe.
Fearing to blink and missing
a move

Should I be a parrot ?
A nice grey empty parrot
That can be stuffed with parrot speak
Wholesome sweet, polite and meek
And just for fun a little cheek.

Who's a pretty polly ?
Oh by golly
Let's be jolly
Let's pretend
Just say nothing
And things will mend.

Who's a pretty polly ?

14th November 2017

There's no need to flap
they're making a map
on which you will see
a touch of the knee
leads up to the gender gap

Sung to the tune of Land of Hope and Glory

Land of grope and horny
It's quite clear to me
Hetro really appals thee
Homo's what you must be.

Rump bump riddle diddle diddle
Rump bump oh

Inappropriate touching's
Going on everywhere
I am in the wrong body
I've been made aware.

So doctor will you change me
I'm not him I'm her?

Rump bump riddle diddle diddle
Rump bump oh

Wilder still and wilder
Paedophiles abound
Rife amongst our long dead
Who're doing it underground.

Rump bump riddle diddle diddle
Rump bump oh

Land of hope and glory
What they doing to thee

12ᵗʰ December 2017

Thirty nine thousand million divided by sixty six million two hundred and
ninety four thousand equals five hundred and eighty eight pounds 29p.

£39,000,000,000 divided by 66,294,000 =   £588.29

It's simple arithmetic, not a trick question, just a suggestion as we all play
suckers and mugs, suckers and mugs.

The folk with dementia know it's a joke but they have to pay, they have to
pay, they have to play suckers and mugs, suckers and mugs. Such happy
suckers, laughing away, what did you say? It's pension day, hooray, hooray,
suckers and mugs, suckers and mugs.

The homeless must pay, the homeless must pay. They're in the game and
they have to play suckers and mugs, suckers and mugs. The fat cats to pay,
the fat cats must play far away, far away the fat cats need plenty, plenty all
day. Empty your pockets the fat cats to pay, the fat cats all play at fritter
away, fritter away. As fat cats they play suckers and mugs, suckers and
mugs.

The students will pay. The students will pay, those being cloned they
groan, they groan the students have loans, give some away, far away the
fat cats need plenty, plenty all day to fritter away, fritter away at suckers
and mugs, suckers and mugs.

The working will pay, the working will pay, give them your life, give them
your wage, give them your freedom, feed them, feed them, give them your
work far away, far away. The fat cats must play far away, far away, the fat
cats need plenty, plenty all day. Give them your pockets to fritter away,
fritter away. Slavishly, slavishly, slaves, slave, slave away we all must play
suckers and mugs, suckers and mugs. We all must play, and all must pay as
they fritter away, fritter away.

The babies will pay, born today, born today the babies will pay, they will
play suckers and mugs, suckers and mugs before they can say suckers and
mugs, suckers and mugs. Fritter away fritter away they'll have to play
they'll have to play slave away slave and fritter away fritter away.

INTRODUCING! *Extract from 'Plonkout Too'*

Eager forward younging, swirling, licking, licking up the spitting of the sky. Passing by the wallowers in want, followers of the leaders, bleeders of the followers as they grovel wallowing in wanting what the leading bleeders hold up as example standard. Lapping up the licking in the low-way through the valleys, swishing, sallying through the alleys, bolder-bordered crumples in the crust of our careering speck of dust. All embracing better, encased within a bubble looking out. The weather's getting wetter but the spirit's so much better getting pleasure from the wetter seeing water all a tumble down the high sides of the valleys as we sally through some settlements of some aborigines.

Like all's a flowing as we're going and the tensionless is showing as the jolly's going solid drawing closer to a blessing-size proportion as we are making motion licking up the spitting of the sky, breezing through the wringing wetter. Good spirit ball is rolling and gathering momentum to become of major moment, let us pray. And to cry we'll have to try as the climate is set fair in the bubble as we bubble, through the wetter swishing, pleasant as a granted wish.

We journeyed through the rugged, through the clammy to a cluttered space, the place of one large clan.

One amongst our number understands their temples and their tokens and the utterances spoken in the rituals of the pagan aborigines. And has studied all the values of the pagan aborigines. So we left her by the shining shrine, the market place, the temple of the lowerarchy aborigines. Left her to her mission with some local tokens studying their icons and continued through the hovels gliding round and left and right through the wetter to a swampy clearing, the land of Hobohemia.

9th January 2018

How can we tickally connect

When it isn't politically correct?

TACITURN

13th February 2018

Speech! **Speech!**

Ifters, Blevers,

Inkum poke papum. Eatly un slogan a gump
a jah.   A gump a jah feep. A gump a jah
slodgem. Slodgem feep, Ifters, Blevers,
slodgem feep.   Rhadi Klingish, shrays,
boveses en pluveses.

Hurber igs zat cur.   Tav, tavro, tavroen.
En ack, en rection.

Leppot nurp en denk, en jonk, mocup a
vilding sop fosp. Roop.   Roop utch,
utching throg, lubbit. Lubbit tong ghin
surrs ro. Suff.   Suftup en cun   ting nicsoc
oove.

Ifters, Blevers

A gump a jah!

First published on a postcard in 1982.

SKETCH OF THE DAY
Tuesday 12/01/'18

Daubs on the horizon,
an impressionist masterpiece
hitting the eye
as ships translate into islands.
An archipelago,
sometimes snow-capped,
appears and goes
as we tack together
towards oblivion.
Krakatoa.

You will fill in the gaps.
Explore, connect the dots
build on it.

There was a toy soldier
Who married a doll
From the same shelf
Of the shop on the mall.

Thus, random atoms
Make one molecule
Joined with vibrations
The glue so cool.

Magical physics
And fizz chemistry
Need not be known
To achieve wizardry.

He was of the band
Of the brave fusiliers
And plays solo horn
When on stand it appears.

Imagine the joys
Awaiting upstream
The baubles and bling
The theme song of dream.

Truly I know of
Adventures ahead
But what I could say
For now, leave unsaid.

13th March 2018

Good Morning Britain.
I had gigabytes for breakfast
with my tablet and tv
which entertained with twinkle twat,
vaginal dryness spray,
and told me of tampons
and pads for catching wee.

There was healthy toilet cleaner
and a toilet-roll for dogs.
The weather's on a high
but forecast not to last.

The news was all abuse
by those heterosexual devils
which was really pretty old hat
being practised by millennials,
long before language
tampered with our base essentials.

How far back will we go?
Do those dark ages lure
with incubi and succubi
the spooks of before?
And psychosis of the cloister
where ignorance held sway
delivering cruel culture
as the only righteous way.
Will the inquisition's perverts
sadistically rise
bestowing masochism
with the holiest disguise?

Will the burkha
marching black and awesome
          obtain the fashion status to obey?
t's all a private matter gone public today.

22

COOL JAZZ

Call it a kind of jazz, cool jazz to excuse, explain this syncopated strangeness as we are on the journey dare we dare to visit that big and wondrous city curiosity, where the serious meets with witty, with the inside-job style intrigue rising up before you.

Will the hope confound the hopeless with the mighty weapon purpose, with its' goal so vital though so trivial on the whole, though rising up before you as we struggle with misunderstanding breaking pots within earshot and attractive cleavage so distracting yet there's fear to speak of, to acknowledge the delighting, pleasing, fearless exposure. Where's the like it button for this come and get it gesture, dare we press it, this retro link, a think to fashion history held in our city curiosity?

And so, giving forgiveness for the shower of the shards having failed to overpower, gone by without a mention as un-noticed. So now how else to draw attention to the hour, and so it's music time to entertain no-one or one and only which is equally abusive to our purpose, unaware or no respect we know not which. We know you're there without contempt whittling at our self-respect, our fearless exposure with determination, cries for help and so daring go past non-disclosure and information freedom legislation.

Thus, another paltry law rises up before us generated by the workless for the fearful has occurred and has lost its purpose, turned worthless as the natural fearless easy obvious escape as laws do not a prison make our minds can liberate from the history we are and living in as we ramble through the city curiosity.

10th April 2018

Deafened by the row
     of yapping dogmas

In the dark but
     not allowed the light

Where we are and why we're here
     we cannot know

But a wise man from the East End
     told me "Mind how you go."

From 'The Roll of the Artist'

I am standing up to my thighs in the sea.
I am facing the shore. A wave gently
creeping towards the beach, climbs my
back, laps around my arm-pits and
continues quietly on to its destination.
I swayed like a firm planted sturdy palm
in the morning sun.

A change of mind is a bit like that.
Thoughts gently and quietly penetrate,
rock us about and can change our stand.

YOU FISHED?

The ground bait issued
fogs
spin the line the bait the lure
payout
reeling
payout
reeling reeling

The snag
jerks shut the lips
hooked on a salary
reeling reeling
into the keep net

8th May 2018

PARAPHRASTICALLY SPEAKING

You can do it
When you promiscuity.

- _ _ _ _ _ _ _ _ _ _ _ _

His eyes and smile and dressing style
Were altogether cool,

And when in bed his hairy head
Was always next to mine.

We cuddled up and snuggled up,
He went with me to school.

We cried and kissed and never missed
Our playtimes hide and seek.

He then one day was put away
For some outrageous crime,

So bad it was I know because
They said don't speak his name.

What had been done to spoil our fun
Is sure the greatest wrong,

As still I find that in my mind
I do so love old golliwog.

From Page 75 'The Tin Book'

There's a cottage by a traffic stream
       that no-one should ignore,
it has decibelic diesel
       stereo-piped to every floor.

And none could fail to pick up
       the articulated vibes
which are felt from top to bottom
       and are known to shake the sides.

In its garden growing
       there's health foods by the bed,
veg that's radiation-proof
       foliage fed the purest lead.

In every way a residence
       ideal for a slave,
for unless compelled to live there
       who could summon so much brave?

SHIPPING FORECAST

Attendance all stripping. The Biological
Society wish you'd follow this morning
and pip emma a plenty true theme
rhyme today.

There is a tale warming and dawning of
stripping for see areas
risqué
Fair Isle, Jersey, unfasten it.
White valley
sillies   bite
ridge dowsing
warm front   high
Mumbles
Wick
sperm point,   Orcock Head
rising steady,   good,
forth,   dogger.

Associated frontal trough
over
try me   Prestwick
liking.
sole,   imminent,
lumpy,
finish there,
soon.

First published on a postcard in 1982.

12th June 2018

COUNTRY LIFE

They picnicked salad on the green,
A picture-perfect family,
In undulating country scene
Of thick hedgerows and shallow ford
With young ones frolicking and free
All harmony and sweet accord.

Until what seemed a change of plan
As dogs and us with little fuss
Were helped into our special van.

Without a care we journeyed on
As down the lanes we bouncing sped
The motor giving urgent song.

There was no husky au revoir
As gentle lovely Daisy-Bell
Stood shitting in the Abattoir.

JOSEPHINE BAKER
14th May '18

A Biographical Villanelle.

With bold Elastic Mattress dance
The Charleston and the Mess Around
One's prone to give in to romance.

And never slow to take a chance
To star her aim whilst on the ground
With bold Elastic Mattress dance.

To Shuffle Along Blackbottoms prance
And Honeysuckles' honkey sound
One's prone to give in to romance.

She left the States and conquered France
Where spirited she lithely clowned
With bold Elastic Mattress dance.

Resistance skill her wartime stance
And should contrariness astound
One's prone to give in to romance.

She gave her whole to woo to trance
And celebrated though un-crowned
With bold Elastic Mattress dance
One's prone to give in to romance.

THE PIPER

Squeeze the bag.
Finger holes.
Swinging kilt.
Tassled balls.

Stiff erect.
Slittings high.
All correct.
A let it fly.

Legs pilose.
Stirrings still.
Buckly hose.
Upper frill.

Pego lowin'.
A sporon pie.
Safety pin.
Wailing cry.

First printed on a postcard in 1981.

10th July 2018

STREETWISE

No work, no worries,
Rich and plenty.
Leisured.
Sleep all day,
Snug and comfy.
Out most nights.
Catch a dinner.
Moonlight.
Slink and swagger,
Pick a fight.
Stalk.
Three a.m.
Choose a target.

The shrieking starts.
Lovely.
The joy.

That's what I do.
Can't help it.
Everybody knows.

They call me Tom.

80% OF EVERYBODY HAS HPV
There are over 100 varieties

Adam in the garden
Full of passion and desire
Was dunking in an oyster
Lovely juices to acquire.
But just as he was happy
With forbidden fruit to grow
There came a suited serpent
With some scientific info.
"I'm obliged", said he, "to tell you
It's the devil of a crisis,
For there's Papillomavirus
Swimming in your gorgeous iris".

THE WAY OF LIFE

Literally it took an eternity to get us here. Really truly an eternity and having got here we struggle to decide what to have for lunch.

It's so important.

Shall we eat in or out? Eating out would save a lot of work. The shopping. The washing up. Eating out would seem like a day off. A holiday. So what shall we do?

It's so so important.

Maybe we're at the very end of eternity. We don't know. But we don't speak of that.

It's far too important.

Yet it could be the last supper. And loaves and fishes come to mind.

To finish the day our work or play we organically pray at the shrine of the great ubiquitous Lord my creator, the great Lord God of fuck.

And we laugh.

It's all so important.

14th August 2018

READING RICHARD

He's looking forward to oblivion
Having peeled and peeled the onion
And found there's nothing there
But more onion.
So he'll stay right on the track
On and on no turning back.

It's oblivion or nothing.

THE DEATHSCAPADE

They danced to the whistle
      and the rattle of the guns
at the celebrated killings
      in Europe of the sons.
And glorious the comings
      at the lustings with the huns.

Let us be ashamed.

They eagerly attended
      The Sarajevo rave,
Sanitized and dressed to kill
      as worthy of the brave
and were ordered, choose mass suicide
      or firing squad to grave.

Let us be ashamed

To eulogise the madness
      Is the madness to compound
As bits of meat and suffer
      Were shaken to the ground,
and within the zings of terror
      unheeded screamings sound.

Let us be ashamed

11th September 2018

THE VISITING BABIES

Yo-yos without strings.
Going, coming back
and round and round.
Nothing found.
Going, coming back
and round and round.
Over here,
over there.
Must be something
somewhere.
Nothing found.

So cry for now.

PATRONISING

Shell-shocked

[handwritten: Bomb bamb ba bomba bomb]

Let's all be nice about it
Let's song and dance about it
What are we doing here?
Be where the atmosphere
Bomb bomb ba bomba bomb
~~Breathe in the air of fear~~ ✓
Father of novichok
Shhh shhhh it's eleven o'clock
Look now at what I've got
Didn't I make a nice poppy
Onion bhagee
Let's all stick together
Make up a theory clever
Hole in the head
~~Professor~~ big shit.
Let's be nice about it
Lets's song and dance about it
Shafted and blasted
It's bloody murder
What about those 'thou shalt nots'
So up spake little strumpet boy
Bayonet sharp
General assistant pc director's assistant's
Blowing her trumpet
Female first female first
Nicely spoken eton sandhurst
Living fossil establishment trained
The parrot pump it
Brain-washed stone-cold soul
So it was it is the same
They don't apply
Not convenient
Suspended for the duration
"If any question why we died
Tell them because our fathers lied"
Bomb bomb ba bomba bomb
Rudyard Kipling
Bomb bomb ba bomba bomb
Mummy mummy
Will it hurt?
When they kill me
Mummy mummy
I want my mummy

[handwritten annotations in margins: sing / Beware / Hiss Hisss / el fresko / BRAND NEW hand new / been / 9 a nice poppy pp / different / BLOWWUP pig shit / bomb bomb b bomba bomba bomb / bomb bomb big bomba bob / FACTOTUM / GENERAL DIRECTORS ASSISTANTS P.C. ASSISTANT FACTOTUM / ASSISTANT / GENERAL DIRECTORS / assistant ASSISTANTS ASIS-ASSIST / bomb bomb ba bomba bomb / dont apply thou shalt nots / dont apply / Kajino without front / bomb bomb ba bomba bomb]

39

9th October 2018

POETRY COMPETITION

Won the prize.
So be told
"This is good".
Are you listening,
Stupid man.

— — — — — — — — — — — —

SESTET

With a love that so disturbs
That a Poet's stuck for words
And can't speak his mind in rhyme
So without romantic line
Told his problem to Jemima
She said, "Could you use vagina?".

1ST DIVISION
VICTIMS UNITED V THE REST

Well, as was expected, starting with dirty
dribbling, it was foul play all the way.
Pandemonium broke out when Victims United
scored first from a corner and then off a
penalty. This was too much for The Rest's right
wing who killed their own goalie on the spot,
hanging him from his own crossbar. Their fans
went hysterical, frantically working their rackets
they chanted,

"Hang him again! Hang him again!"
Whilst the Victims crowd rolled in the terraces
laughing.

There followed the fanciest ever football. The
ball was soon nowhere to be seen and long
before half-time they kicked each other to
death.

From 'The Tin Book'

GRANDMAMA

She lived in the alms houses known as the guilt
complex.
A colourful character she had blue legs,
Said incest was a family affair.
Said she wasn't wild about HPV, but it grows on you.

Her table setting was a knife, fork, spoon
And a pair of scissors to cut up her salad.

Divorced of course. The grounds were quite
comprehensive,
Subtly described as every 'conceivable' reason
Embracing a multitude of sins.

Grandpa said she insisted on a king-size bed
In case we had visitors.

Printed in Poland
by Amazon Fulfillment
Poland Sp. z o.o., Wrocław

65576329R00026